THE MANIFEST PRINCIPLES

Aligned. Activated. Abundant.

Christine Zanjanipour

DETAILS MATTER BOOKS

ISBN: [Insert ISBN here]
First Edition

Published by Details Matter Books

Printed in the United States of America

For more information, visit:
[www.DetailsMatterBooks.com]

To my beloved sons, Kai and Skyler.

 You have always carried these principles within you—
seeing with clarity, dreaming with imagination,
and believing with a faith that moves mountains.

The world will open to you
as much as you dare to claim it.
And I know you always will.

With endless love,
Mom

Table of Contents

Part Three – Your Guided Journey

Introduction

When I Didn't know Manifesting was Called, "Manifesting"

Ever since I was a young girl, I had an unshakable sense that if I could clearly envision a situation, an achievement, or even a simple moment—I could bring it into my reality. I didn't know at the time that there was a name for this ability; I just believed.

In 1974, my parents moved our family into a home in Southern California's San Fernando Valley, once owned by Mickey Rooney and his fourth wife, Elaine. The house itself was large, but what mattered most to me was the swimming pool, a setting for many childhood memories. Every summer, I would race the neighborhood kids, and before each competition, I'd close my eyes and picture my hand being the first to touch the pool's edge. Time after time, that visualization became my reality. My mantra then, as it is now, was simple: "just believe."

As I grew, so did my understanding—and the stakes. Whether it was acing a challenging test, landing a dream job, or planning an exotic vacation, I noticed that clearly envisioning the outcome often led it to manifest in my life. It wasn't until 2006, when I read The Secret by Rhonda Byrne, that I realized this "gift" had a name: manifesting.

Manifesting has shaped every chapter of my adult life, from attracting the husband and family I envisioned, to creating a lifestyle and home in Colorado's Rocky Mountains. Along the way, I also learned that manifesting works both ways—what you focus on, positive or negative, can come to pass. A vivid example: years ago, while kayaking the Colorado River with my husband, Alex, I became fixated on the fear of flipping my kayak in the cold, rushing water. Sure enough, my fears materialized, and I found myself upside down in the icy current. That

1

experience taught me the importance of consciously redirecting my thoughts toward what I want—rather than what I fear.

Now, I invite you to join me as we explore the seven principles of manifesting. Together, we'll uncover how to harness this power to create the life you truly desire.

The Manifest Principles Manifesto

We are creators of our own reality.
We choose clarity over confusion, belief over doubt, and alignment over resistance.
We honor the journey as much as the destination.
We trust the process, knowing that each step taken in inspired action leads us closer to what we seek.

We release what no longer serves us and make space for the new.
We embody our truest selves, fully and unapologetically.
We remain open to receiving in all forms, recognizing that abundance flows when we allow it.

We are part of something greater than ourselves—co-creators with the Universe.
Together, we hold the power to shift, to rise, to expand, and to flourish.
The Manifest Principles are not just words on a page, but a way of living—moment by moment, choice by choice.

This is our commitment. This is our manifesto.
And by choosing it, we choose ourselves.

We speak clearly because we know the Universe is listening.

The History of Manifesting

Manifesting has existed for centuries, woven into the teachings of ancient civilizations, spiritual traditions, and modern-day psychology. From sacred texts to philosophical works, the idea that our thoughts, beliefs, and energy influence our reality has always been present. Ancient Egyptians, Greek philosophers, and Eastern spiritual traditions all explored the power of the mind and its connection to the universe.

In more recent history, manifesting evolved through movements such as New Thought, the Law of Attraction, and quantum theories of consciousness, blending spirituality with science. Today, it continues to grow in relevance as people all over the world recognize that their inner world directly impacts their outer experience.

The story of manifesting is not just history—it's a living practice, available to you in this very moment. As you turn these next pages, remember that every word, every exercise, and every principle is here to empower you. This is your invitation to step into possibility, to rewrite what you believe is possible, and to begin creating the life you've always imagined.

Let's start this journey now. If you lean in with an open heart and a curious mind, these pages have the power to change your life.

Part One: The 7 Manifest Principles

Introduction to the Principles

Manifestation is not magic—it is mastery. It is the art of aligning your inner world with your outer reality, of living from intention instead of reaction. But intention alone is not enough. Without structure, desire remains hazy. Without principles, dreams scatter like seeds tossed into the wind with no soil to catch them.

That is why the Seven Principles exist. They are not rigid rules, but guiding forces—pillars that anchor your vision in the physical world. Together, they form a map: from the clarity of knowing what you want, to the belief that it is possible, to the emotional alignment that magnetizes it, to the inspired actions that bridge thought and form, to the detachment that frees energy, to the identity shift that sustains it, and finally, to overcoming resistance so that nothing blocks the flow.

Each principle builds on the last. They are sequential, but also cyclical. You may revisit them many times as your desires evolve. Think of them as a dance with the Universe—a rhythm you learn, step by step, until it becomes second nature.

And so we begin where all creation begins: with clarity.

Principle One: Clarity

Clarity is what the Universe responds to

Clarity is not a luxury; it is the foundation of manifestation. Without it, our energy scatters like light through a fog. With it, intention sharpens into a laser beam. The Universe is responsive, but it is not random. It is like an echo chamber, reflecting back exactly what you broadcast. And what you broadcast is determined by how clearly you know what you want.

Too often, we move through life with vague hopes rather than precise visions. We say we want "more money," "a better relationship," or "to feel happy," but these declarations are not blueprints—they're placeholders. "More money" could mean an extra $200 a month or complete financial freedom. A "better relationship" could mean greater intimacy, or simply fewer arguments. Happiness could mean adventure for one person and stability for another. When we're unclear, we send scrambled signals. And the Universe, always faithful in its responsiveness, mirrors that back: mixed results, partial successes, fleeting glimpses of what we desire.

Clarity is the bold act of saying, This is it. This is what I want. It requires self-permission, vulnerability, and courage. Because once you name your desire specifically, you risk judgment. You risk disappointment. But you also ignite power. Clarity is magnetism in its purest form.

The Illusion of Safety in Vagueness

Vagueness feels safe. If we never name what we truly want, then we never have to face the sting of not getting it. It protects us from judgment: no one can laugh at our dreams if we never say them aloud. But the safety of vagueness is an illusion. In truth, it keeps us locked in limbo.

Imagine walking into a restaurant and saying to the waiter, "Bring me something good." Perhaps you'll get something edible, but will it be what you crave? The chef cannot prepare your favorite dish if you won't name it. The Universe works the same way. Vague desires create vague results.

When you get specific, you might worry that you're being "too much." Too demanding, too unrealistic, too bold. But the opposite is true. The Universe thrives on precision. When you say, "I am ready for a partner who is kind, adventurous, and deeply committed," or "I am calling in a role where I make $200,000 a year leading creative teams," or "I am creating a life where my mornings begin in spacious peace," you send a frequency that is crisp, undeniable, and magnetic.

The Courage to Want

Clarity begins with permission. Permission to admit what you want. Permission to say it aloud. Permission to want more than others think you deserve.

From childhood, many of us were taught to dim our desires. "Don't be greedy." "Be realistic." "You can't have everything." Those messages often left us cautious with our dreams. We watered them down, made them more palatable, kept them "reasonable."

But clarity requires you to remove the filter. Wanting is not greed. It is guidance. Desire is your soul's compass. The things that light you up are not random—they are invitations into the fullest expression of who you came here to be.

Ask yourself: If I could wave a magic wand and no one would judge me, what would I ask for? That is the voice of clarity.

Peeling Back the Layers

Sometimes, what we think we want isn't ours at all. We inherit desires from culture, family, or society. The sprawling house, the prestigious job, the luxury car—maybe those aren't true desires but borrowed scripts of what "success" should look like.

True clarity requires excavation. You must peel back the layers of conditioning and ask:

- Where did this desire come from?
- Does it feel alive for me, now, in this season of my life?
- Does it excite me—or simply feel familiar?

Perhaps you've been chasing the corner office because it was expected of you, when your heart actually longs for freedom and creativity. Maybe you thought you wanted the suburban house, but what you really crave is community

and nature. Clarity requires ruthless honesty. And that honesty is liberating.

Tools for Gaining Clarity

Journaling for Truth

Set aside time with a journal and ask yourself:

- If failure were impossible, what would I pursue?
- What have I been too afraid to admit I want?
- What do I pretend to want, but secretly don't?
- What am I done tolerating?

Write without censoring. Let the answers spill out. Often the deepest truths reveal themselves in the sentences we almost didn't write.

Visioning Exercises

Close your eyes and imagine your ideal day in vivid detail. Where are you waking up? Who is with you? What does your body feel like? What do you spend your hours doing? Visioning bypasses logic and speaks directly to the soul.

Declaring It Aloud

There is immense power in speaking desires into the air. Words shift energy. Say it aloud as if you're ordering from the cosmic menu: "I am ready for a home filled with light and peace." "I am calling in work that feels meaningful and abundant." Speaking turns clarity into declaration.

Navigating Fear

Clarity will often stir fear. The fear of disappointment: What if it doesn't happen? The fear of judgment: What will people think? The fear of success: Can I handle it if it does happen?

These fears are normal. They are signs that you're stepping beyond your comfort zone. But remember: disappointment is temporary, while regret is permanent. People will judge no matter what—better to be judged for living boldly than for hiding. And success? Success is safe. You are more capable than you realize.

Clarity as Alignment

Clarity is not simply about naming desires. It is about aligning with them. It is saying to yourself and the Universe: This is mine. I am ready. I am willing to walk toward it.

When you choose clarity, the Universe listens. Opportunities, synchronicities, and people begin to align in ways you could not have orchestrated. You don't need to know the "how." You only need to know the "what."

Affirmations for Clarity

- I fully authorize myself to want what I want.
- My clarity is magnetic.
- I release the "shoulds" and honor what I truly desire.
- The clearer I become, the faster life aligns.
- I trust that knowing what I want is enough—the how will follow.

Living the Principle: Clarity

I have countless examples of how clarity has shaped my path, but one of the earliest—and most defining—came at the very beginning of my career. At the time, I was working for a company that had just announced an opening in their New York City office. I had never even been to New York, but the very thought of the big city set my heart racing. The energy, the possibility, the skyline—I could feel its magnetic pull even from miles away.

With a mix of excitement and nerves, I walked into my boss's office and asked to be considered for the position. To my surprise, he didn't dismiss me. Instead, he told me to take the weekend to think carefully about it and report back on Monday.

That weekend became a turning point. I didn't just "think about it." I lived it. In my mind, I was already there. I saw my apartment in vivid detail, the way I'd decorate it, the city-chic furniture, the little touches that would make it my sanctuary. I imagined the clothes I would wear, feeling the confidence of someone who belonged in Manhattan. I pictured myself walking among the tall buildings, swept up in the unstoppable rhythm of the city. I could hear the cabs honking, feel the rush of people moving with purpose, and smell the roasted chestnuts from a street cart in autumn.

One vision lit me up: strolling through Central Park in the fall, leaves crunching underfoot, the crisp air carrying the unmistakable hum of New York. I could see my family visiting me, their wide-eyed wonder as I took them to Broadway shows, iconic landmarks, and little hidden gems I'd discover as a local.

By the time Monday rolled around, I wasn't "considering" the idea anymore. I was already there. In my mind, I had made the leap, and my energy reflected that certainty. When I sat down with my boss again, I spoke with conviction because I wasn't asking for the opportunity—I had already claimed it.

Two months later, I was unpacking boxes in my New York City apartment. Everything I had envisioned, the space, the lifestyle, the feeling of belonging—was now my reality.

That experience taught me one of my most powerful lessons: when you are clear in your vision, when you see and feel every detail as if it's already yours, the Universe moves quickly to meet you there. Clarity doesn't just guide you—it transports you.

Closing

Clarity is not about perfection. It is about courage. It is the bold step of saying: This is what I want, and I am ready to claim it. When you choose clarity, you step into alignment with your highest self. And in that alignment, manifestation begins.

The Universe is listening. Speak clearly

Transition to Principle #2: Belief

You've taken the first step—you've named what you truly want. You've peeled back the layers of conditioning, silenced the outside noise, and listened to the quiet, unwavering voice of your soul.

But clarity alone isn't enough to bring a vision to life.
Desire without belief is like planting a seed and then refusing to water it.
The next step is to anchor into a truth so deep it lives in your bones: Not only is what you want possible—it's already on its way to you.

In the coming chapter, we'll explore the alchemy of belief—how to shift from hoping to knowing, from wishing to expecting, and from visualizing to becoming the version of you who already has it.

Your clarity lit the spark.
Your belief will turn it into an unstoppable fire.

Principle Two: Belief

Belief is the bridge between desire and reality

Clarity plants the seed. Belief is what waters it. You can know exactly
what you want, describe it in vivid detail, even declare it every day—but
if somewhere deep inside you doubt it's possible, the signal weakens.
Clarity without belief is like a blueprint without a builder: the vision
exists, but nothing rises from it. Belief is the force that transforms desire
into inevitability. Without it, dreams remain ideas. With it, those same
dreams become destiny.

Nature of True Belief

Belief is often misunderstood. Many think it means blind optimism,
pretending everything is fine even when it isn't. But true belief is not
about ignoring reality. It's about choosing which reality you empower.
Belief is deciding that your vision is more powerful than your
circumstances. It's not about pretending your challenges don't exist—it's
about knowing they cannot overrule your future.

Belief is a posture. A stance. A way of saying, Even before I see it, I
know it's mine.

Think back to a moment when you believed so deeply in something that
doubt didn't even register. Maybe you applied for a job and somehow
just knew it was yours. Maybe you met someone and instantly felt they'd
play a pivotal role in your life. Maybe you pulled into a crowded parking
lot and knew—without question—a space would open right where you
needed it. That unshakable knowing is belief. And it is that vibration the
Universe responds to.

The Conditioning of Doubt

From childhood, we are conditioned to believe only what we can see. We're told to be "realistic," to lower our expectations, to avoid disappointment by not dreaming too boldly. We learn to wait for evidence before allowing belief.

But manifestation works the opposite way. The Universe doesn't say, "Prove it, then I'll deliver." It says, "Believe it, and I'll match your frequency."

This is why belief feels risky. It asks you to stand in certainty when there's no proof yet. It invites you to live as if something is already true when the physical world hasn't caught up. But that's exactly the bridge: in the space between clarity and reality, belief is the ground beneath your feet.

The Conscious vs. Subconscious Divide

Here's the tricky part: what you say you believe isn't always what you truly believe. Consciously, you may affirm, "I believe I'm worthy of love." But unconsciously, you may carry the wound of rejection that whispers, "I am too much" or "not enough." Consciously, you may declare, "I believe in abundance." But each time you check your bank account, your nervous system tightens, rehearsing lack.

This gap between conscious desire and subconscious programming is where most people get stuck. Belief must live not only in your words but in your body, your emotions, and your energy. Closing that gap is the work.

How Belief Is Built

Belief is like a muscle. At first, it may feel weak, shaky, or even artificial. But muscles grow through repetition, and so does belief.

- Repetition: The subconscious does not shift through logic alone—it shifts through consistent exposure. Affirmations, journaling, and repeated visualization train the mind to accept a new reality. At first, saying "I am worthy" may feel hollow. But say it, write it, embody it enough times, and the subconscious begins to absorb it as truth.
- Incremental Growth: You don't have to leap from 0% belief to 100% certainty overnight. A spark is enough to start. Even if you believe just 2% more today than you did yesterday, you are moving the needle. That spark, nurtured, becomes a flame. That flame, tended, becomes a wildfire.
- Borrowed Belief: If your faith feels thin, borrow belief from others. Read stories of those who achieved what you desire. Surround yourself with expanders—people who embody what you're moving toward. Their certainty can carry you until yours grows strong enough to stand on its own.

Belief as a Daily Choice

Ultimately, belief is not passive—it is a choice. Each morning, you choose which reality to align with: the one shaped by fear or the one guided by faith.

It might sound like this:

- Today, I choose to live as if my vision is already true.
- Today, I choose to act like the person who has what I want.
- Today, I choose to trust that what I desire is already in motion.

Each choice compounds. With time, those choices solidify into certainty. Your energy sharpens, your actions align, synchronicities appear, and opportunities open.

The Paradox of Belief

Here's the paradox: you don't need unshakable certainty to begin. You only need enough belief to take the next step. Life meets you there. When you step forward with imperfect but willing faith, the Universe supplies confirmation in the form of aligned opportunities. Those confirmations strengthen your belief, which magnetizes even more.

You don't need to "fake it" until you make it—you only need to step forward with what you have and let it grow.

Practices for Strengthening Belief

Affirm with Emotion: Pair affirmations with feeling. Don't just say "I am abundant." Feel what abundance would feel like. This locks belief into your body.

Act As If: Align your actions with your desired identity. Want to be healthy? Start making the choices your healthiest self would make—even in small ways.

Catch Contradictions: Notice when your words and energy don't match. Gently reframe. Instead of "I'll never figure this out," say, "I'm in the process of figuring it out."

Celebrate Evidence: Keep a "proof journal." Record synchronicities, blessings, and answered prayers. Over time, this collection becomes undeniable evidence that reinforces belief.

Affirmations for Belief

- I trust that what I desire is already on its way.
- Each day my belief grows stronger.
- My vision is more powerful than my circumstances.
- Doubt is natural, but faith is my choice.
- Belief is the bridge—and I am crossing it boldly.

Living the Principle: Belief

Belief has always been my favorite principle. Maybe it's the actress inside me, but there's something magical about fully stepping into the role of already having what you desire — before it shows up in your reality. Belief isn't passive hope; it's active embodiment. It's walking, talking, and carrying yourself as though the thing you want is already yours.

One of the clearest examples from my life came during my senior year of high school. We had just moved to a new city, which meant starting over at a brand-new school. At first, I wasn't thrilled about leaving behind the friends I had grown up with since elementary school. But as the year unfolded, I discovered unexpected gifts: new friends, new opportunities, and classes I never would have experienced otherwise.

My favorite class quickly became Speech. I loved the creativity of writing and the energy of delivering clever, heartfelt speeches. Toward the end of the year, an announcement was made: auditions were being held for graduation speakers. The moment I heard it, something inside me lit up. I knew, without hesitation, that this was mine.

Of course, the idea of speaking in front of hundreds of people carried a mix of nervous excitement. But here's the key — before I ever wrote a single word, before I even signed up for an audition, I believed so strongly that I would be chosen that I began preparing as if it were already true. I didn't just picture myself on that stage — I felt it. I could see what I would wear, how I would style my hair and makeup, even the exact moment my name would be announced. I rehearsed my speech over and over, not from a place of hoping, but from a place of knowing.

When audition day arrived, I walked into that room full of faculty with absolute certainty. Delivering my speech felt effortless, almost like I was stepping into a role I had already been living for weeks. I didn't just believe I could be chosen — I believed I was the speaker.
And then, just days later, the announcement came: my name had been chosen as the commencement speaker.

Looking back, I realize it wasn't just the words of my speech that secured my spot — it was the belief. The unwavering knowing that I already had what I was reaching for. That is the essence of this principle: belief bridges the gap between desire and reality.

Closing

Belief is not about perfection—it's about persistence. It's the willingness to stand on the bridge even when the fog of doubt surrounds you. It's knowing that your desire was not placed in your heart by accident—it was planted with purpose.

Clarity gives the Universe the blueprint. Belief is your declaration: I trust this blueprint is being built, even if I can't see the construction yet.

Cross the bridge with confidence. Life is already waiting for you on the other side.

Transition to Emotional Alignment

When you believe you're worthy of your desires, something powerful happens — the door opens. But belief alone isn't enough to keep that door wide and the path clear.

The next step is learning to live in the energy of what you want.

Because while your beliefs shape the blueprint, it's your emotions that bring it to life. They are the current running through your manifestation, the vibration the universe actually responds to.

You can believe with your mind, but if your emotional state is sending a different signal — one of fear, doubt, or scarcity — the message gets scrambled.

That's where emotional alignment comes in. It's the art of feeling now the way you'll feel when your desire arrives and letting that emotional state become your new normal.

Let's explore how to tune your inner GPS so your emotions guide you straight toward the reality you're calling in.

Principle Three: Emotional Alignment

"Your emotions are the frequency that tunes your reality."

If clarity tells the Universe what you want, and belief carries you across the bridge of possibility, then your emotions are the fuel that draws your desire toward you. You cannot manifest joy from despair, freedom from fear, or abundance from scarcity. The frequency you hold most consistently is the one life reflects back to you.

We are emotional beings. Every thought sparks a feeling, and every feeling becomes energy. That energy radiates outward like a broadcast signal, announcing your vibration to the Universe. When you align with emotions that match your desires—gratitude, excitement, peace, love— you become magnetic. Opportunities, people, and synchronicities are drawn into your orbit, not because of luck, but because your frequency is in harmony with your vision.

Emotional alignment is not about pretending to feel good all the time. It's about cultivating awareness and choosing, moment by moment, to steer yourself toward emotions that support your vision. Sometimes the shift is subtle—a breath, a smile, a new thought. Sometimes it's profound—releasing grief, forgiving, or choosing joy after hardship. What matters is your willingness to notice where you are and consciously turn your dial toward where you want to be.

Emotions as a Compass

Your emotions are not random—they are guidance. Think of them as the compass of your soul. When you feel expansive, joyful, or grateful, you are aligned with your true desires. When you feel anxious, resentful, or constricted, you're receiving feedback that your focus is misaligned. This does not mean emotions are "good" or "bad." Every feeling has value because it reveals where your energy currently sits. Even so-called "negative" emotions are signals—indicators that your perspective or focus is out of sync with your highest self. Instead of resisting these feelings, you can acknowledge them, thank them for the guidance, and gently pivot toward emotions that serve your vision.

The Frequency of Creation

Imagine a radio dial. Each station broadcasts at a different frequency. If you want to hear jazz but you're tuned to rock, you won't get the music you desire. Manifestation works the same way: your emotions set your dial.

- If you want love but vibrate with fear of abandonment, you're on the wrong frequency.
- If you desire prosperity but dwell on lack, you're tuned to scarcity.
- If you long for freedom but live in worry, you're aligned with restriction.

Your task is to adjust your emotional dial to match the outcome you desire—before it arrives. You don't wait until money shows up to feel abundant; you generate the feeling of abundance now. You don't wait for love to arrive before feeling cherished; you embody the vibration of love in your daily life.

When your emotions align with your desires, you begin broadcasting the frequency of already having it—and life responds in kind.

Emotional Set Points

Most people operate from an "emotional set point"—a baseline mood they return to again and again. For some, it's anxiety. For others, cynicism. For others still, it's hope or optimism. This set point is usually shaped by early conditioning and repeated experience.
The good news is, it is not fixed. Just as you can train a muscle, you can elevate your emotional baseline through practice. Gratitude journaling, meditation, breathwork, laughter, and intentional joy practices can shift your set point upward. Over time, emotions like peace, gratitude, and joy can become your default.

Stories of Emotional Alignment

- The couple who found their dream home: After months of frustration with real estate showings, they decided to stop focusing on the lack and instead began practicing gratitude for their "dream home." Each evening they envisioned the joy of living there. Within weeks, a home that matched every detail appeared, and their offer was accepted against heavy competition.
- The woman who called in love: For years she lived in loneliness, repeating the belief, No one ever chooses me. She began shifting her emotions by practicing self-love rituals: buying herself flowers, speaking kind words to her reflection, and feeling adored in her meditations. Soon after, she met her partner—not because she chased harder, but because her frequency shifted to I am loved.
- The entrepreneur who dissolved money fear: Though his business grew steadily, his anxiety about finances held him hostage. He began practicing daily gratitude for the clients and money he already had. Over time, his emotional alignment shifted from fear to trust, and with it, his revenue expanded.

These stories reveal the same truth: emotions magnetize outcomes. Align your emotional energy, and the external world reshapes itself around you.

A Gift of Alignment

When I was about twenty years old, my dad told me about this miracle little prayer called *The Prayer of Jabez*.
He said it was powerful — that it had changed lives.
So I memorized it.

"Oh that You would bless me indeed,
and enlarge my territory,
that Your hand would be with me,
and that You would keep me from evil,
that I may not cause pain."

I didn't fully understand it back then — but I said it anyway. Sometimes quietly. Sometimes out loud.
And over the years, it became a rhythm in my life.

These days, I usually remember to say it when I'm driving.
There's something about the open road — just me, the sky, and those words — that makes it feel alive.
I say it with conviction, joy, and gratitude.
And almost without fail, miracles follow.
Opportunities appear. Doors open. Divine timing unfolds.

I can't explain how it works — I just know that it does.
Maybe that's what "enlarge my territory" really means — not about having *more*, but *becoming more*.
More open. More trusting. More aligned.

The Story Behind the Prayer of Jabez

The Prayer of Jabez appears quietly in the Bible — in **1 Chronicles 4:9–10** — tucked between a long list of names.
Most verses just mention who begot whom, but suddenly the story pauses. Because Jabez was different.

It says he was "more honorable than his brothers,"
and that his mother named him *Jabez,* meaning *pain,* because she bore

him in sorrow.
So from the very beginning, his life carried a label — *pain*.

But Jabez didn't let that define him.
He prayed boldly:

"Oh that You would bless me indeed,
and enlarge my territory,
that Your hand would be with me,
and that You would keep me from evil,
that I may not cause pain."

And then — the verse ends with six simple, miraculous words:

"And God granted his request."

That's it. No fanfare. Just faith answered.

The story of Jabez reminds us that no matter how we begin, or what pain
we carry, we can ask for expansion — for life to stretch us into greater
purpose.
It's not a prayer for wealth or status.
It's a prayer for *alignment*.
A willingness to say: "I'm ready for more — not out of fear, but faith."

Reflection from Christine

To me, this prayer *is* emotional alignment — the merging of belief, trust,
and divine timing.
It invites the Universe to meet you halfway.
It calls in the unseen hand that guides, protects, and expands your life in
ways you couldn't plan if you tried.

This prayer was a gift from my father.
Now — it's my gift to you.

Take a deep breath.
Say it aloud.
Feel your heart open as you do.
And then — watch what happens next.

Journal Prompt:

Where in my life am I ready for divine expansion?
What would it look like if I trusted that the Universe could "enlarge my territory" in ways beyond my imagination?

The Science of Emotion

Modern science echoes this ancient wisdom: emotions are energy. They alter brainwave states, release chemical messengers, and change the electromagnetic field around your heart. Research from the HeartMath Institute shows that elevated emotions like love, gratitude, and compassion create coherence—synchronizing your physiology, boosting health, and broadcasting measurable signals outward.

In other words, when you feel better, you don't just feel better—you broadcast better. The world responds to that frequency shift. Practices for Emotional Alignment

1. Awareness Check-ins: Ask throughout the day, How do I feel right now? Does this feeling align with what I want?
2. The Next Best Feeling: If you can't leap from fear to joy, aim for a gentler shift—like relief, neutrality, or hope. Each small step matters.
3. Emotional Anchors: Create triggers that bring you back to alignment—uplifting music, calming scents, joyful movement, or affirmations.
4. Emotional Rehearsal: Visualize your desired reality and feel its emotions as though it's already here. This conditions your nervous system for alignment.

5. Embodiment: Move your body to shift energy. Dance, walk, breathe deeply—remember, emotion is energy in motion.

Emotional Integrity

True alignment doesn't mean plastering a smile over pain. It means honesty. If sadness arises, feel it. If anger comes, honor it. But don't live there. Emotions are meant to move. Feel fully, then consciously pivot toward states that serve your vision.

This balance prevents toxic positivity and anchors you in authentic alignment.

Affirmations for Emotional Alignment
- I honor every emotion as guidance.
- My emotions are my compass, and I choose the direction of my dreams.
- Gratitude, joy, and love flow through me daily.
- I align with the frequency of my desires now.
- My emotions magnetize the reality I want.

Living the Principle: Emotional Alignment

Emotional Alignment is all about tuning your inner state to match the reality you want to create. It's not just thinking about your dream — it's feeling it, living it inside of you before it exists outside of you. When your emotions vibrate at the same frequency as your desires, the universe rushes in to meet you.

For me, one of the most powerful demonstrations of this principle was our move to Colorado.

I had always loved skiing, while my husband Alex had been a passionate snowboarder for most of his life. When our boys, Kai and Skyler, were just six and seven, we started taking them on snowboard trips across the country. It didn't take long before they were flying down mountains with confidence, and before we knew it, our family tradition of "snowboard safaris" was born. Over holiday breaks, we'd pack up the car in Dallas and head off to three or four different resorts. Inevitably, Colorado became our favorite. The mountains there held a magic that we couldn't shake.

After every trip, Alex and I would look at each other and say, "Someday, we're going to move to Colorado." We said that for nearly ten years. But the truth was, every time we said it, we weren't just speaking it — we were feeling it. Each visit planted the emotional seeds of our future life.

Then, during Kai's senior year, we took a road trip to visit universities in Colorado. One afternoon, while strolling the streets of Aspen, it hit us like a wave. That old "someday" we had been carrying in our hearts suddenly turned into today. In that moment, we both felt it deep in our bones: we were going to move to Colorado.

We didn't know how it would all work. Colorado was far more expensive than Dallas. Alex wasn't sure what he would do for work. I didn't know if my company would allow me to live outside of my sales territory. We didn't know what our house would sell for, or how Skyler, still in high school, would feel about leaving. The list of unknowns was endless. But none of that mattered — because the emotional decision had already been made.

When we returned home, we immediately started preparing to sell our house. I created a vision board of our Colorado life and even wrote our new mailing address on an envelope, just to feel the reality of it. I looked up local grocery stores, dentists, and even hair salons, as though I were already living there. Every step was fueled by that emotional alignment — living in the feeling of already being a Colorado family.

The biggest question mark was my job. I scheduled a meeting with my boss, Melissa, to share our plan and ask if I could work remotely. The meeting kept getting delayed, which only heightened my nerves. I played the conversation over and over in my head, trying to calm the anxiety with the vision of what I wanted.

Finally, while sitting in a rental car in a rainy Miami parking lot during a business trip, the meeting happened. My heart raced as I told her, "Melissa, Alex and I want to move to Colorado." There was a long pause — the kind that feels like an eternity. And then she said with a little laugh, "Well, who doesn't?"

In that instant, the tension dissolved, and I knew our dream was becoming real. Not only did Melissa approve of my move, she also promoted me to Director.

That was the power of emotional alignment in action. Long before we knew the details, we lived the feeling of our Colorado life. And because we aligned emotionally with it, the path opened. To this day, I carry immense gratitude for Melissa Morman, whose belief in me made the transition possible.

Emotional Alignment is about becoming the vibration of what you desire — not someday, but today. When you live from that place, the "how" reveals itself.

Closing: The Art of Feeling First

Manifestation is not about waiting for evidence before you allow yourself to feel good. It's about choosing to feel good first. When you generate gratitude, love, and joy now, you magnetize more reasons to feel them later.

You don't manifest what you say you want—you manifest what you consistently feel.

So ask yourself each day: What emotion aligns with my desires? And how can I generate that feeling right now?

Choose joy. Choose gratitude. Choose trust. And watch as life arranges itself to match the music of your heart.

Transition to Inspired Action

When your emotions are aligned, you move through life in harmony with your desires rather than in resistance to them. But alignment isn't just about feeling good—it sets the stage for what comes next: taking action. Not all action is created equal. There's a vast difference between effort born from struggle and force, and action that flows naturally from your aligned state. The former drains you; the latter propels you. This is where the power of Inspired Action emerges—the bridge between inner alignment and outer manifestation.

Principle Four: Inspired Action

"Aligned action is the bridge between energy and form."

Manifestation is not a passive game of waiting—it is a dance between vision and movement, between alignment and action. Clarity gives you direction, belief sustains your faith, emotions fuel your vibration. But without action, your desire has no channel through which to arrive.

The key is not any action, but inspired action. Ordinary action is often forced, frantic, or fear-driven. It's rooted in the belief that if I just do enough, push enough, hustle enough, I'll make it happen. Inspired action, however, flows from alignment. It feels like a nudge, a spark, a pull from within that says, this is the next step.

Inspired action is not about struggle. It is about moving with clarity, trust, and energy that feels alive. It is less about doing more and more about doing what matters most.

The Nature of Inspired Action

How do you know the difference between forced action and inspired action?

- Forced action feels heavy, urgent, pressured. It's fueled by fear of what might happen if you don't act.
- Inspired action feels light, guided, exciting—even if it stretches you outside your comfort zone. It carries an undertone of curiosity and flow, not panic.

You can spend months in busywork that looks productive but creates no real results because it is not aligned. Or you can take one inspired step that collapses timelines, opening doors you could never have forced open.

The Inner GPS of Inspiration

Your intuition is your built-in GPS for inspired action. When you are emotionally aligned, intuitive guidance becomes louder and clearer. You might feel it as a hunch, a sudden idea, a pull toward a conversation, or even a random thought that keeps resurfacing.

The Universe rarely hands you the entire map. Instead, it reveals the next step. Inspired action is about saying yes to that step, even if you don't yet see the whole path.

Stories of Inspired Action

- The phone call that changed everything: An author struggling to land a publisher felt a nudge to reach out to an old colleague. That colleague happened to know an agent looking for exactly her genre. One email led to a book deal that transformed her career.
- The career leap: A man dissatisfied in his corporate job kept journaling about freedom and creativity. One morning, he felt an urge to sign up for a weekend workshop in photography. That single step led to connections, freelance work, and eventually a thriving business.
- The move that made space: A couple seeking a new home felt overwhelmed by the market. Instead of forcing endless searches, they followed a gentle nudge to declutter their current apartment. Within weeks, their dream home appeared—because their inspired action created energetic space for it.

Why Inspired Action Matters

Energy alone is not enough. Without channels, energy stagnates. Action gives the Universe avenues through which to deliver. Think of it as electricity: belief and emotion generate the current, but action is the wiring that carries it into form.

At the same time, hustle without alignment scatters your energy. You can exhaust yourself chasing, but if your actions are not inspired, they only reinforce struggle. Manifestation is not about doing everything—it's about doing the right things, at the right time, in the right energy.

Practices for Cultivating Inspired Action

1. Tune In Daily: Begin your morning with stillness. Meditate, journal, or simply breathe. Ask: What would my future self do today? Write down what arises.
2. Follow the Nudges: Don't dismiss the small whispers—make the call, write the post, attend the event. Often the smallest steps carry the biggest momentum.
3. Release the "How": Your role is not to orchestrate every detail, but to follow the next aligned step. Trust the bigger picture will reveal itself.
4. Check the Energy: Before acting, ask: Am I moving from fear or from trust? From pressure or from joy? If it feels forced, pause. If it feels inspired, move.
5. Celebrate Movement: Every inspired action, no matter how small, is a declaration of trust. Celebrate the step itself, not just the outcome.

The Balance of Effort and Flow

One of the biggest misconceptions in manifestation is that you must either "hustle endlessly" or "sit back and wait." Inspired action is the middle path. It acknowledges that you are a co-creator. You bring energy into motion, and the Universe responds with synchronicities, opportunities, and connections.

Think of it like rowing a boat in a river. Forced action is paddling furiously against the current. Passive waiting is dropping your oars and drifting aimlessly. Inspired action is aligning your boat with the flow of the river and rowing with steady, purposeful strokes.

Affirmations for Inspired Action

- I am guided to the perfect next step.
- My actions are aligned with my vision.
- Inspiration flows to me and through me.
- I trust the nudges of my intuition.
- Every step I take moves me closer to my desire.

Living The Principle Inspired Action

A few years ago, I had this strong, almost irrational pull to start baking sourdough bread. At the time, it didn't make "logical sense." I was busy with my career, my calendar was full, and I could have easily dismissed it as a distraction. But something inside whispered, "This matters. Follow it."

So, I bought a small jar, started a sourdough starter, and began experimenting. At first, my loaves were flat, under proofed, or too dense. But I kept going because the process lit me up. There was joy in the rhythm of kneading, waiting, and sharing loaves with friends and neighbors.

Here's the key: I didn't know why I was doing it—I just felt guided to keep at it. That's what inspired action feels like. It's not about certainty; it's about alignment.

Fast forward: that little "nudge" grew into something much bigger. It became a new brand idea, "Flourishing Bread Co," a class business, and a way to connect with people through food and community. Something that started as a quiet spark turned into a path I never could have planned if I'd sat down and "strategized."

Looking back, I see that inspired action isn't about having the whole plan figured out. It's about trusting the small, aligned steps, even if they don't seem significant at the time.

Closing: The Power of the Next Step

You don't need to know every step of the journey. You only need to say yes to the one that's in front of you. Inspired action compounds—each step reveals the next, and together they carry you into alignment with your vision.

The Universe meets movement. When you take inspired steps, you signal your readiness, your trust, and your willingness to participate in your own creation.

Clarity sets the direction, belief builds the bridge, emotion fuels the energy. But it is action—inspired action—that carries you across the threshold from vision into reality.

Transition to Detachment

Taking inspired action opens doors, creates momentum, and signals to the universe that you are ready. Yet, once you've taken the step that feels aligned, there comes a crucial shift. If you cling too tightly to outcomes, you begin to choke the flow you've set in motion. Manifestation requires both movement and surrender. You plant the seed with clarity, water it with belief and action, and then allow it the space to grow. This is the paradox: the more you try to control the "how" and "when," the more resistance you create. That's why the next principle—Detachment—is the art of releasing control while still trusting deeply in your vision.

Principle Five: Detachment

"Letting go is what allows the Universe to move."

After clarity, belief, emotional alignment, and inspired action, comes a principle that feels paradoxical—detachment. It is, without question, one of the most challenging steps in manifestation. At first glance, it seems counterintuitive. If I've poured my heart into defining my desire, believing in it, aligning with it emotionally, and taking inspired action, shouldn't I cling to it until it shows up?

The truth is: clinging creates pressure, and pressure creates resistance. Detachment is not about abandoning your desire; it is about releasing the desperate grip on when, how, or through whom it arrives.

The Seed Metaphor

Imagine planting a seed in fertile soil. You carefully prepare the ground, water it, and give it sunlight. Then—what do you do? You walk away, trusting nature's timing. You do not dig it up every morning to see if it has sprouted fast enough. You don't shout at it to hurry. You don't demand evidence every hour. You know that growth is happening beneath the surface.

Detachment is exactly that. You've planted the seed of your desire through clarity, belief, emotions, and action. Now you step back. You let the process unfold.

The Energetic Weight of Attachment

Attachment radiates lack. When you grip tightly, your energy says: I don't have this yet, and I need it now. That vibration stems from fear—fear of missing out, fear of unworthiness, fear of failure. Fear creates resistance, and resistance blocks flow.

Detachment radiates trust. It says: I know this is mine in some form, and I don't need to micromanage the how or when. That energy is open, spacious, receptive. It allows the Universe to orchestrate details in ways your limited perspective could never have designed.

Allowing vs. Controlling

The opposite of allowing is controlling. Control is the ego at work—the part of you that insists outcomes must unfold on your terms, in your timing, in the packaging you prefer. But manifestation is not a solo act; it is a co-creation.

Your role is to set the vision, align your energy, and take inspired steps. The Universe's role is to weave unseen threads, connect the dots, and deliver opportunities. When you overstep into control, you choke the process.

Allowing, by contrast, is expansive. It means trusting life to surprise you with something even better than you imagined. It is the willingness to say: This or something better.

The Paradox of Letting Go

Here is the paradox: the moment you release your desperate need for your desire, you become magnetic to it.

Think of times in your life when you wanted something so badly it consumed you—yet it seemed just out of reach. And then, the moment you let go—when you shifted your focus, relaxed, or stopped obsessing—it appeared. The job, the relationship, the unexpected check in the mail.

This is not coincidence. It is energetic alignment. Detachment dissolves resistance, creating space for receiving.

Why Detachment Feels Hard

We are conditioned to believe that holding tighter leads to success. Culture equates effort with worthiness and struggle with value. Letting go feels risky, even irresponsible. It feels like surrendering control—and in a way, it is.

But surrender is not failure. It is wisdom. It is recognition that force often delays what flow can deliver with ease.

The difficulty of detachment lies in trust. To release control, you must trust something bigger than yourself. And trust feels vulnerable in a world that prizes certainty. Yet without trust, manifestation stalls.

Detachment Is Not Apathy

Let's be clear: detachment is not about saying, I don't care if this happens or not. True detachment is passionate but peaceful. It means you care deeply about your desire, but you don't suffocate it with constant neediness.

It's the difference between hovering over your planted seed and letting it bloom in its own time.

Detachment does not lessen your desire—it enhances your ability to receive it.

Stories of Detachment

- Love Arrives Unexpectedly: A woman spent years anxiously seeking a relationship. Every date was charged with fear: Is he the one? When she finally shifted her focus to joy, hobbies, and self-love, she released attachment. Months later, she met her partner—effortlessly, without force.

- The Business Breakthrough: An entrepreneur obsessed over landing a single client, convinced their business depended on it. Their energy was tense and needy, and the client pulled away. When the entrepreneur let go—trusting that opportunities were abundant—another client appeared, larger and more aligned than the first.

Again and again, life proves: when you loosen your grip, miracles move in. Read this again.

The Practice of Detachment

Detachment is a skill. Here are practical ways to cultivate it:

1. Shift from Need to Preference: Instead of I need this, say I would love this, but I trust it's this or something better.
2. Release Timelines: Trust divine timing. Often, desperation for speed delays the process.
3. Anchor in Gratitude: Gratitude roots you in abundance now, easing the pressure of what hasn't yet arrived.
4. Play with Possibilities: Stay curious. Ask, How else might this unfold? Curiosity dissolves rigidity.
5. Return to Trust: Remind yourself: What is meant for me cannot pass me by.

Affirmations for Detachment

- I release control and trust the process.
- What is meant for me arrives with ease.
- I care deeply, but I no longer cling.
- I allow the Universe to surprise me.
- I am open, receptive, and free.

The Emotional Freedom of Letting Go

Detachment liberates you. It releases you from the heavy chains of need and desperation. You stop bargaining with the Universe, stop demanding evidence every hour, stop living in anxiety.

Instead, you find peace, presence, and joy in the now. And ironically, that freedom is what magnetizes your desires. You stop chasing. You start attracting.

Living the Principle: Detachment

I once applied for what I thought was my dream job. I prepped for the interviews, visualized myself in the role, and wanted it so badly that I could almost taste it. But after the final round, I got the call: they chose someone else.

At first, I was crushed. My mind kept spinning with why not me? But then something shifted. I realized that if this door was closed, it wasn't meant for me—and maybe something better was on its way. Instead of forcing, I released it. I decided to detach from the outcome and focus on what I could control: showing up fully where I was, continuing to grow, and trusting the bigger picture.

A few months later, an even better opportunity landed in my lap—one I never could have orchestrated myself. Looking back, I see how detachment wasn't about "giving up" on what I wanted. It was about releasing the grip, trusting that the right thing would align at the right time, and making space for something even greater to arrive.

Closing: Trusting the Timing

One of the deepest lessons detachment teaches is trust in timing. The Universe is never late. Sometimes, delays are not denials—they are preparation. The house you didn't get, the job that didn't come through, the relationship that fell apart—all may be clearing the path for something better.

When you detach, you send this message: I trust. I am safe. I know this or something better is coming.

And from that trust, the Universe delivers—often in ways more magical than you ever imagined.

Transition to Identity Alignment

When you practice detachment, you release the tension that comes from grasping at outcomes. You've declared your desire, taken inspired steps, and surrendered the timeline. What's left is the most powerful work of all—shaping who you are at the core. Manifestation isn't just about asking or waiting; it's about aligning your inner identity with the reality you want to experience. You cannot hold onto the identity of "someone waiting" and expect to receive—you must embody the person who already lives the life you've envisioned. This leads us into the next principle: Identity Alignment, where desire transforms into being.

Principle Six: Identity Alignment

"You don't manifest what you want—you manifest who you are."

At the heart of manifestation lies a profound truth: your identity is the engine behind your reality. Desires are magnetic, yes—but they cannot override the self-image that governs your choices, your expectations, and the way you move through the world. You may dream of abundance, love, or freedom, but if you still see yourself as someone who struggles, someone unworthy, or someone trapped—you will unconsciously keep manifesting versions of that identity.

Identity alignment means embodying the version of yourself who already lives the life you desire. It is becoming the person who naturally attracts, receives, and sustains your vision. Manifestation is not only about what you want—it is about who you are willing to become.

The Power of Self-Concept

Every human being carries a self-concept: a subconscious framework of who you are, what you deserve, and what is possible for you. Most of us rarely question it—it runs quietly in the background like software, shaping how we show up in the world.

Your self-concept is built over time. Childhood conditioning, cultural narratives, and past experiences weave together to form your identity. If your story has always been, I'm the one who struggles, or I'm not the chosen one, or Good things don't last for me, then even when opportunities arrive, you will unconsciously sabotage or push them away.

The subconscious doesn't lie. It will always seek to confirm your dominant identity. That is why lasting manifestation requires not just a change in thought, but a shift in identity.

Becoming the Future You

The key question of identity alignment is: Who do I need to be for this desire to feel natural?

- If your vision is financial abundance, who is the version of you who earns, manages, and enjoys money with ease?
- If your desire is love, who is the version of you who feels deeply worthy of intimacy and partnership?
- If your dream is freedom, who is the version of you who confidently makes choices from sovereignty instead of fear?

The future you already exists—in potential. Identity alignment is about collapsing the gap between that version and who you are now. It's about stepping into their mindset, their habits, their way of showing up—today.

Think of an actor preparing for a role. They don't simply memorize lines; they become the character. They walk like them, think like them, embody their energy. In the same way, manifestation accelerates when you begin living as if you already are the version of yourself who has your desire. Life then organizes itself to mirror your self-concept.

Small Shifts, Big Results

Identity shifts don't require overnight reinvention. Often, they start with subtle but consistent changes:

- Language: Do you speak as someone who is waiting, or someone who is already becoming? Instead of "One day I'll be successful," say, "I am building success now."

- Habits: Does your daily routine match the identity you desire? The "wealthy" version of you might save, invest, and give generously. The "healthy" version of you might choose nourishing foods and joyful movement.
- Boundaries: Who you believe yourself to be dictates what you tolerate. As your identity rises, you naturally stop accepting less than what aligns with your worth.

Over time, these micro-shifts rewire your subconscious. What once felt like "trying on" a new identity becomes second nature.

Releasing Old Identity

Stepping into a new identity requires releasing the old one. And this can feel like grief. Even painful identities—the struggler, the victim, the over-worker—can feel familiar, and therefore safe. But clinging to an outdated version of yourself keeps you locked in outdated manifestations.

Ask yourself: What story about myself am I still carrying that doesn't belong to my future?

Perhaps it's the story of being the one who has to work harder than everyone else. Or the one who never gets chosen. Or the one who always has "just enough." Honor those versions—they got you here. Then release them with gratitude, making space for your becoming.

The Embodiment Practice

One of the most powerful practices for identity alignment is embodiment. Each morning, visualize your future self. See what they wear, how they walk, the way they carry themselves. Feel their calm, their confidence, their joy.

Then ask: What would this version of me do today?

- Would they negotiate differently?
- Would they speak with more confidence?
- Would they prioritize self-care?
- Would they say no to what drains them?

Then—do that thing, however small. Embodiment collapses the gap between "future me" and "present me." You stop waiting for change to prove you are different. You become different, and change reflects that.

Affirmations for Identity Alignment

- I am already becoming the version of me who lives my desires.
- My choices, words, and actions align with my highest self.
- I release identities that no longer serve my becoming.
- I embody my future self here and now.
- Who I am is aligned with what I attract.

Living The Principle Identity Alignment

For a long time, I had ideas swirling in my head—cookbooks, manifestation guides, hospitality books. I would jot notes, play with outlines, and dream about them, but deep down I still saw myself as someone *trying* to become a writer rather than already being one. That gap between who I thought I was and who I wanted to be created resistance.

The shift happened when I stopped focusing on the outcome and instead fully stepped into the identity. I began telling myself: *I am an author. I am a publisher. I am a creator of books that change lives.* I started living as if that were already true, and everything began to change.

Once I aligned with that identity, writing became effortless. It was no longer about forcing myself to sit down and "get something done." It felt natural, like part of my everyday rhythm. I created **Details Matter Books** as the home for my work, and instead of thinking about just one book, I suddenly saw the bigger vision: a whole catalog of works. *The*

Manifest Principles, Manifest Principles in Business, I Am Because I Say I Am, The Hostess with the Mostest, and more.

Each completed draft and each published book wasn't just a milestone to check off—it was proof that my new identity was real. I no longer questioned whether I was a writer; I had become one. And because my actions flowed from that identity, they didn't require the same kind of willpower. I was simply being who I already knew myself to be.

Looking back, I realize I didn't wait until my books were finished to call myself an author. I claimed the identity first, and the results flowed naturally from there. That is the power of alignment—when who you *say you are* matches what you believe and how you live, success becomes inevitable.

And the ripple effect of that shift has been powerful: the same alignment fuels everything I create—whether it's writing, baking, hospitality, or building lifestyle brands. Once I embraced the identity of a creator, every venture I touched became an extension of that truth.

Closing: Remembering Who You Really Are

Identity alignment is the bridge between possibility and inevitability. When you live as the person who already has what you desire, manifestation stops being a chase and becomes an expression of who you naturally are.

And here is the deeper truth: manifestation is not about pretending—it's about remembering. Your soul already knows who you are meant to be. When you align your identity with that knowing, you stop forcing, doubting, and hustling. You allow life to reflect back the truth you've embodied: I already am.

Transition to Overcoming Resistance

When your identity is aligned with your desires, you begin to embody the version of yourself who naturally attracts what you seek. This alignment creates power, confidence, and clarity. Yet even with this inner shift, life has a way of testing your resolve. Old patterns resurface, limiting beliefs whisper their doubts, and external circumstances may seem to push back against your vision. These moments aren't signs of failure—they're invitations to rise higher. To manifest fully, you must learn how to meet resistance with awareness rather than fear. That is why the next principle—Overcoming Resistance—is essential: it teaches you how to transform obstacles into stepping stones on your path to creation.

Principle Seven: Overcoming Resistance

"What you resist not only persists—it expands."

Resistance is one of the greatest obstacles to manifestation. It is the invisible wall that keeps your desires at arm's length, no matter how clear, aligned, or inspired you are. You may know what you want, believe it's possible, feel the emotions, take action, and even embody the identity of your future self—and yet, something seems to stall. That "something" is usually resistance.

Resistance is not failure. It is simply friction. It is the energetic static that comes from fear, doubt, old conditioning, or inner conflict. Think of it like driving a car with the emergency brake on. You are still moving forward, but with unnecessary strain. Release the brake, and suddenly the same effort takes you farther, faster, with greater ease.

What Resistance Looks Like

Resistance takes many forms, some obvious and others subtle:

- Self-doubt: "Who am I to have this?"
- Fear of failure: "What if I go for it and it doesn't work?"
- Fear of success: "What if it works, and I can't handle it?"
- Unworthiness: "I don't deserve this."
- Overthinking: Endless analysis instead of movement.
- Procrastination: "I'll do it later…" (but later never comes).
- Perfectionism: "It has to be flawless before I start."

At its core, resistance is protective. The subconscious mind resists because it thinks it is keeping you safe. Safety to the ego often means staying in the familiar, even if the familiar is painful.

The Energetics of Resistance

Resistance creates a push-pull dynamic. On one hand, you are calling something in; on the other, you are energetically repelling it. The result is stagnation, mixed signals, or stop-and-go manifestations.

This is why it often feels like two steps forward, one step back. Desire pulls you ahead, while resistance pulls you back into old patterns.

But here's the liberating truth: resistance is not a dead end. It is a mirror. Whatever you resist reveals the beliefs, fears, or stories still asking to be healed.

Meeting Resistance with Awareness

The first step in overcoming resistance is awareness. You cannot transform what you refuse to acknowledge.

Begin noticing where resistance shows up:

- Do you feel tension in your body when you think of your desire?
- Do you sabotage progress right before a breakthrough?
- Do you find yourself waiting for the "perfect" moment?
- Do you cling to the belief that it has to be hard?

Instead of shaming yourself, meet resistance with compassion. Resistance is not your enemy; it is your teacher. It is pointing to the exact place within you that is ready for liberation.

Releasing Resistance

There are many ways to soften and release resistance. Here are some of the most powerful:

1. Acknowledge the Fear. Resistance is often rooted in fear. Name it. Say, "I am afraid of failing," or "I am afraid of being seen." Naming dissolves its hidden power.
2. Reframe the Story. Ask: Is this belief actually true? Often, resistance is built on outdated stories. Challenge them. Replace "I'm not ready" with "I am growing into readiness every day."
3. Breathe Into It. The body holds resistance as tension. Breathwork, meditation, or even a few slow inhales and exhales release energy and calm the nervous system.
4. Take Micro-Actions. Resistance thrives on overwhelm. Break your desire into small, doable steps. Each small action builds momentum and dismantles fear.
5. Shift from Control to Trust. Much resistance comes from trying to force or predict outcomes. Surrender the "how" and "when." Remind yourself: I trust divine timing. What is meant for me cannot pass me.

Resistance vs. Flow

When resistance softens, flow returns. Flow feels like synchronicity, ease, and expansion. It is when opportunities come seemingly "out of nowhere," when people appear at the right time, when you feel carried rather than burdened.

Think of water flowing around rocks in a river. Resistance is the rock. Awareness and release are what allow the current to carry you forward anyway. Over time, even the largest boulder is smoothed by the flow of water.

Stories of Overcoming Resistance

- The artist who feared visibility. She longed to share her work but resisted posting online, fearing criticism. Once she acknowledged the fear and reframed it as "my work inspires those who are ready for it," she began sharing small pieces. Within months, she built a community that adored her.
- The entrepreneur afraid of success. Every time his business grew, he found himself procrastinating, missing deadlines, or avoiding new clients. Deep down, he feared that success would mean burnout. When he released that belief and redefined success as easeful, he doubled his revenue without working harder.
- The woman resisting love. She claimed she wanted partnership, yet every time someone got close, she pulled away. She realized she was still carrying the story that love equals betrayal. By healing that wound, she opened to connection—and love entered her life with grace.

Practices for Releasing Resistance

- Journaling Prompts:
  - Where am I holding back out of fear?
  - What story am I telling myself that no longer serves me?
  - What would it feel like to let go of control and trust?
- Daily Mantras:
  - I release the need to control outcomes.
  - I trust the process of life.
  - Resistance is leaving my body and mind.
  - I am safe to receive what I desire.
- Embodiment Ritual:
  Stand tall, shake out your body, and say aloud: "I release resistance. I allow flow." Move your body freely for a few minutes, letting energy shift.

Living The Principle Overcoming Resistance

When the idea for *Flourishing Bread Co.* came to me, resistance was quick to follow. My mind immediately threw up roadblocks: *Do I really need to create another brand? Will people understand what I'm trying to do? Is this going to be too confusing, too much, too different?* That inner voice of doubt tried hard to keep me in hesitation.

But there was something powerful about this idea that I couldn't ignore. *Flourishing Bread Co.* wasn't just about bread. Yes, it's inspired by the art and symbolism of bread, but it's also about flourishing in life. Bread represents nourishment, community, and also prosperity—"bread" as money, abundance, and success. I realized I wasn't simply creating a brand; I was planting the seeds of a movement that tied together everything I believe in: growth, manifestation, and the details that matter in life.

Instead of letting the resistance hold me back, I leaned into the vision. I started shaping what this movement could stand for. I imagined a book that blended recipes with life lessons, a lifestyle brand that carried messages of abundance, and even products that reminded people daily of what it means to flourish. The more I allowed myself to expand into the idea, the more the resistance lost its grip.

What felt heavy at first became exciting the moment I shifted my perspective. I stopped seeing resistance as a sign to quit and started seeing it as proof that I was on to something meaningful. Resistance shows up most when we are about to step into alignment with a bigger vision. For me, *Flourishing Bread Co.* was exactly that—a vision that merged my creativity, my love of food, and my passion for inspiring people to flourish in every area of their lives.

Looking back, I realize that overcoming resistance wasn't about eliminating fear—it was about moving forward despite it. The moment I chose to honor the double meaning of bread—both nourishment for the body and prosperity for life—I gave myself permission to expand. What once seemed risky started to feel inevitable, as though it had been waiting for me all along.

Flourishing Bread Co. isn't just a brand—it's a movement, a reminder that we are all capable of rising, expanding, and creating abundance in every form. And for me, pushing past resistance was the first step in proving that truth to myself.

Reflection & Takeaway

Resistance is often the loudest right before a breakthrough. It tries to disguise itself as doubt, fear, or hesitation, but its presence usually means you are standing at the doorway of something powerful. The lesson I learned through *Flourishing Bread Co.* is that resistance is not a stop sign—it's a compass pointing directly toward growth. When you choose to step through it, you don't just overcome fear; you unlock a new level of possibility, one that was always waiting on the other side.Closing: The Gift of Resistance

Here is the paradox: resistance is not here to stop you—it is here to refine you. Each time you meet it, you grow stronger, more aligned, and more resilient. Each time you soften into flow, you expand your capacity to receive.

When you stop fighting resistance and instead learn from it, you reclaim your power. You realize that nothing outside of you is blocking your manifestation—it is only the inner friction asking to be released.

Overcoming resistance is not about force; it is about surrender. It is the willingness to say: I trust. I allow. I am ready.

And in that surrender, the path clears. The brake releases. And manifestation, once heavy and slow, begins to feel effortless, natural, and inevitable.

Closing Thoughts on Part One

These seven principles are your foundation. Clarity sets your vision. Belief builds the bridge. Emotional alignment fuels the signal. Inspired action moves the energy. Detachment allows the flow. Identity anchors the new self. Resistance tests and strengthens your path.

Together, they form the architecture of manifestation. Return to them often. Practice them daily. Embody them deeply. With these as your foundation, everything you desire has room to arrive—and stay.

Part Two: Applying The Principles

Part Two Introduction

In Part One, we uncovered the foundation of manifestation—understanding clarity, belief, and the inner framework that shapes every outcome in your life. That section gave you the awareness and language to see how manifestation is not random luck, but an intentional process that begins with who you are at your core.

Now, in Part Two, we move from insight to embodiment. This is where the concepts you've learned become actionable, where principles turn into practices that can reshape your daily reality. Here, we explore the energetic alignment required to bring your vision into form—your emotions, your actions, your identity, and the way you interact with resistance.

Think of this section as the "living laboratory" of manifestation. It's no longer about theory or wishing—it's about integrating these truths into your decisions, your habits, and your way of being. Each principle in Part Two builds upon the last, giving you the momentum to shift from thinking about what you want to actually becoming the person who creates and sustains it.

This is the activation phase—the moment where clarity transforms into courage, intention evolves into movement, and your desires start to take shape in the world around you.

Step 1

Harness the Power of Belief to Turn Desire into Knowing

Belief is the soil in which every dream is planted.
Without it, the most brilliant ideas and heartfelt desires wither before they have the chance to take root. With it, even the smallest seed of possibility can grow into something extraordinary.

When you think about what you want — the home, the relationship, the career, the feeling of freedom — it begins as a spark of desire. But desire alone is not enough. If your belief is shaky, the energy you send out is mixed. The Universe responds not to what you say you want, but to the vibration you actually hold. Belief is the bridge between wanting something and living it.

In this chapter, we move beyond "hoping it happens" into the realm of knowing it's already yours.

Why Belief Is the Fuel of Manifestation

Everything you manifest is filtered through your sense of what's possible for you. If deep down you believe you can only achieve "just enough," then "just enough" is all you will experience. If you truly believe in limitless abundance, your reality begins to shift to reflect that truth.

Belief shapes perception, and perception shapes reality. This isn't just metaphysics — it's psychology, neuroscience, and energy all working together.

Your brain is a meaning-making machine. It will seek out evidence to confirm whatever you believe. This is known as the confirmation bias. If you believe "good things always happen to me," you will start to notice opportunities, kindness, synchronicities — and your energy will draw in more of the same. If you believe "nothing ever works out," you'll unconsciously find ways to sabotage yourself and overlook the opportunities right in front of you.

Belief is not static — it's something you can build, stretch, and strengthen like a muscle.

From Desire to Knowing

There are three energetic stages in moving from wanting something to knowing it's already yours:

1. Curiosity – "Could this be possible for me?"
2. Belief – "I know this is possible for me."
3. Embodiment – "This is who I am, and it's already done."

The shift happens when belief becomes so integrated that your mind and body respond as though your desire has already manifested. Your actions, choices, and energy naturally align with the reality you're calling in.

Building Unshakable Belief

Belief is not blind faith. It's choosing to stand in a truth you can feel, even before the physical evidence arrives. Here are steps to make your belief rock-solid:

1. Anchor to Past Evidence

Look back at the times you've manifested something — big or small. The parking space that opened up at the perfect time. The unexpected check in the mail. The job offer that came out of nowhere.
These moments are proof that manifestation works for you. Start a

"Belief Journal" where you record these wins, no matter how small. Your mind needs reminders.

2. Immerse in Possibility

Surround yourself with stories, people, and environments that reflect the reality you want. Read about others who have done what you desire. Spend time with those who inspire you. This expands your subconscious reference points for what's possible.

3. Create a Sensory Blueprint

Belief strengthens when it has something tangible to attach to. Imagine your desire as though it's here now — see it, hear it, smell it, taste it, touch it. The more senses you engage, the more real it feels.

4. Flip the "Yeah, But..."

Every time you catch yourself thinking "Yeah, but that could never happen for me," pause and rewrite it: "Yes, and here's why it will happen for me." Repetition rewires doubt.

5. Act from the Belief Now

If you believed your dream life was already on its way, what would you do today? How would you carry yourself? What decisions would you make differently? Live from that place now, and your belief will grow with every aligned action.

Daily Practices to Strengthen Belief

- Morning Belief Activation: Before getting out of bed, repeat: "I fully trust that what I desire is already mine." Visualize living it.

- Evidence Scan: End each day by writing down three things that proved your desires are coming closer.
- Belief Affirmations: Create personal affirmations that feel expansive but believable. Example: "Every day, I see more proof of my dreams coming true."
- Belief Embodiment: Once a week, dress, speak, and move as the version of you who has already achieved your desire.

Journal Prompts

1. What beliefs have helped me manifest in the past?
2. Which limiting beliefs am I ready to release?
3. What new belief will I commit to strengthening this month?
4. If I truly believed my desire was guaranteed, what would I start doing today?

Affirmation

"I am a powerful creator. I believe in the certainty of my desires, and my reality shifts to match my knowing."

Closing

Belief is the heartbeat of manifestation. When you master it, you'll notice life responding to you in faster, more aligned ways. Opportunities will seem to find you. Synchronicities will multiply. And the bridge between wanting and having will shorten — sometimes in ways that will leave you speechless.

From here, the next step is to become the version of you who naturally attracts what you desire — and that's where we're headed next.

Step 2

Shift Your Identity So You Naturally Embody the Version of You Who Has What You Want

Belief is the seed — but identity is the soil in which that seed grows.

You can believe in a possibility all day long, but if you still see yourself as the person who doesn't have it yet, you'll unconsciously act in ways that keep you aligned with the old version of yourself. Manifestation works best when your internal identity — who you believe you are — matches the external reality you're creating.

Why Identity Shapes Reality

We don't manifest what we want; we manifest who we are.
This is why someone can affirm, visualize, and make vision boards yet still feel like they're "stuck" — their outer actions are at odds with their self-image.

Your identity operates like the operating system on a computer. You can try to run new programs (habits, affirmations, vision work), but if the OS isn't updated, the old programming keeps running in the background. Eventually, it overrides the new input.

Changing your life requires changing your sense of self.

The Identity Gap

When you desire something, there's a space between where you are and where you want to be — the Identity Gap.

- Current Self: The version of you with current beliefs, habits, and standards.
- Desired Self: The version of you who already lives the reality you want.

Shifting your identity is about closing that gap until the you now and the you with your desire are one and the same.

Three Core Shifts to Align Identity

1. Language Shift – Speak as though it's already part of who you are. Replace "I'm trying to be…" with "I am…"
2. Behavior Shift – Make decisions from the perspective of your desired self, not your current limitations.
3. Environment Shift – Surround yourself with cues and reminders that affirm your new identity.

Future Self Embodiment

One of the most powerful tools for shifting identity is Future Self Embodiment — acting "as if" you are already that person. Not pretending, not faking — remembering that this is who you truly are, and letting it show.

Exercise: A Day in the Life of Future You

- Wake up tomorrow and decide you are already living your new reality.

- Ask: "What would Future Me wear? Eat? How would they walk into a room? How would they respond to challenges?"
- Move through your day with that energy — and notice how people and circumstances respond.

Identity Audit

To shift identity, you need to know where you're starting from.

- Beliefs: What do I believe about myself that no longer serves me?
- Habits: Which daily actions reinforce the old version of me?
- Standards: Where am I settling for less than I truly want?

Replace each with beliefs, habits, and standards that match your desired identity.

Breaking the "Someday" Cycle

When you say, "When I have X, I'll be Y," you put your identity shift on hold. Reverse it: "When I become Y, I will naturally have X."
The change happens internally first — the manifestation follows.

Read This Again.

Daily Practices to Anchor a New Identity

- Identity Statements: Write "I am…" statements that reflect your desired self and read them daily.
- Micro-Choices: Ask before each decision: "Which choice would Future Me make?"
- Visual Triggers: Use vision boards, photos, or objects that remind you of your new self every time you see them.

Journal Prompts

1. Who do I need to become to live the life I want?
2. What would my days look like as this version of me?
3. Where am I still acting from the old identity?
4. What single shift can I make today to align with my future self?

Affirmation

"I embody my future self now. My thoughts, choices, and actions align effortlessly with the life I am creating."

Closing

When you shift your identity, manifestation stops being something you "do" and becomes something you naturally are. The gap between dreaming and living your desires closes, and life begins to reflect your new self-image with remarkable speed.

From here, we step into something even more expansive — learning to co-create with consciousness itself. That's where magic meets the tangible, and it's the heart of Chapter 3.

Step 3

Co-Create with Consciousness in a Way That Feels Both Grounded and Magical

Manifestation isn't about forcing your desires into existence; it's about partnering with the creative intelligence that already flows through everything — including you. This partnership is what I call co-creation with consciousness.

When you shift from "I have to make this happen" to "I'm working with the universe to bring this forward," you release strain and open to inspired action. You stop wrestling with life and start dancing with it.

The Two Forces of Creation

Every creation is the result of a dual force:

- You — your intentions, beliefs, energy, and actions.
- The Field — the invisible, intelligent energy that responds to your vibration and aligns circumstances in ways you could never predict.

When you bring these together in harmony, manifestation feels effortless. You move from grind to flow.

Grounded + Magical: The Sweet Spot

Too grounded, and you only rely on logic, leaving no room for miracles. Too "magical," and you may drift into fantasy without creating tangible change.

Co-creation means walking the line — using your practical, grounded self to take real steps, while allowing your intuitive, magical self to guide the path.How to Step Into the Co-Creation State

1. Set a Clear Intention
   Your desire becomes a lighthouse for the universe. The clearer you are, the easier it is for the field to respond.
2. Feel It Now
   Tune into the emotional state of already having it. This is your vibrational match.
3. Release the Timeline
   Let go of when and how it comes. This creates space for unexpected magic.
4. Act on Inspiration
   When a nudge, idea, or opportunity arises — move. These are the universe's breadcrumbs.

The Language of the Universe

The universe doesn't speak in words — it speaks in energy, synchronicities, and symbols.

- A book falls off the shelf.
- A stranger says exactly what you needed to hear.
- A sudden "coincidence" connects you to a perfect opportunity.

The more aware you are, the more these moments appear.

Practice: Daily Co-Creation Ritual

- Morning Alignment: Upon waking, close your eyes, breathe deeply, and connect to the feeling of already living your desire.
- Midday Check-In: Ask, "What's the most aligned action I can take right now?"
- Evening Gratitude: Acknowledge at least one sign, synchronicity, or aligned event from the day — no matter how small.

Over time, this rewires your nervous system to expect support from the universe.

When It Feels Like Nothing Is Happening

Even when you can't see results, the field is rearranging circumstances behind the scenes. Your role is to keep showing up in alignment — not to dig up the seed to check if it's growing.

Trust that your part is to plant, water, and nurture… and the universe's part is to make it bloom.

Journal Prompts

1. How do I know when I'm in "force" mode instead of co-creation?
2. What evidence do I already have that the universe is responding to me?
3. What signs and synchronicities have I ignored in the past?
4. Where can I leave more space for magic in my process?

Affirmation

"I am in a constant dance with the universe. I trust its timing, follow its guidance, and welcome miracles into my everyday life."

Closing

When you start seeing the universe as a partner rather than a distant power, manifestation becomes a collaboration. You do your part, it does its part, and together, you create something greater than you could alone.

Next, we'll explore a principle that strengthens this dance even further — how to practice detachment and allowing without losing momentum. This is where you learn to hold your desires lightly, yet powerful

Step 4

Practice Detachment & Allowing Without Losing Momentum

One of the most paradoxical truths in manifestation is this:
The moment you release your tight grip on a desire is often the moment it finally flows in.

This isn't about giving up — it's about letting go of the pressure. Detachment is not apathy. It's confidence. It's knowing, at a deep level, that what you want is already in motion and doesn't need you hovering over it to "make sure" it happens.

The Energy of Holding Too Tightly

Imagine planting a seed and then digging it up every day to check if it's growing. That's what energetic attachment feels like. You're constantly watching the clock, scanning for evidence, and trying to force the timeline.

Attachment energy is rooted in lack:

- "I don't have it yet."
- "What if it never comes?"
- "What if I lose it when I get it?"

This frequency communicates doubt to the universe, and doubt slows momentum.

What Detachment Really Is

Detachment is emotional freedom from the outcome. It's being in such certainty that your desire is yours, you can relax into the process.

Detachment says:

- "I know it's on its way."
- "I trust it will arrive at the perfect time."
- "I don't need to control the path."

The Power of Allowing

Allowing is the active counterpart to detachment. Where detachment lets go, allowing opens up.

When you allow, you:

- Stay present to opportunities.
- Let the universe surprise you with better than you imagined.
- Remain receptive to guidance, rather than pushing through your own rigid plan.

How to Detach Without Losing Momentum

1. Set It, Then Shift Your Focus
   State your intention clearly, visualize it fully, and then redirect your attention to living your life now.
2. Stay in Action, But Loosen the Grip
   Keep taking aligned steps without obsessing over results.
3. Create Joy in the Present
   The more fulfilled you are right now, the less you'll cling to the future for your happiness.
4. Trust Delays as Redirection
   If it hasn't arrived yet, it's either still aligning or something even better is on the way.

The Science of Letting Go

From a neuroscience perspective, detachment calms your nervous system. When you're in high stress over a desire, you're actually in survival mode — and survival mode is terrible for creativity, intuition, and noticing synchronicities.

By relaxing your focus, your brain shifts into a more resourceful state, making you more receptive to inspiration and opportunity.

Practice: The Release Ritual

- Write your desire on a piece of paper in present tense ("I am so grateful for…").
- Hold it in your hands, feeling gratitude as if it's already here.
- Place it somewhere meaningful (a journal, a special box) and commit to not revisiting it for 30 days.
- Spend those 30 days living as though it's inevitable.

Journal Prompts

1. Where am I gripping too tightly to an outcome?
2. What might happen if I truly trusted the process?
3. How can I bring more joy into the present moment while I wait?

Affirmation

"I release the need to control, knowing my desires are already on their way. I trust, I allow, and I receive."

Closing

When you blend detachment with allowing, you create the perfect environment for manifestation — an open, receptive space where the universe can deliver without resistance.

Next, we'll explore how to design magnetic environments that make it effortless for your desires to find you. This is where your surroundings start working as part of your manifestation team.

Step 5

Design Magnetic Environments That Call in Your Desires with Ease

Your environment is not neutral.
It's either quietly supporting your desires — or quietly undermining them.

Every object, color, sound, scent, and energy in your space is influencing your thoughts, emotions, and actions. If you've ever walked into a room and instantly felt lighter, more inspired, or more at peace, you've experienced the power of a magnetic environment.

When you design your surroundings with intention, they become active participants in your manifestation process.

Why Environment Matters

Your environment is constantly giving cues to your subconscious mind. If your surroundings reflect limitation, clutter, or chaos, they reinforce an inner state that matches those things.

On the other hand, an environment that reflects abundance, clarity, and beauty naturally raises your vibration and keeps you in alignment with your desires.

Think of your space as a vision board you can physically walk into every day.

The Three Layers of a Magnetic Environment
1. The Physical Layer – What you can see, touch, and interact with.
2. The Energetic Layer – The emotional and vibrational "feel" of your space.

3. The Symbolic Layer – The deeper meaning behind what's in your space.

When all three layers are aligned with your vision, you're living in an environment that literally pulls your desires toward you.

The Physical Layer

- Declutter ruthlessly. Clutter represents stuck energy. Every item you keep should earn its place by being useful, beautiful, or meaningful.
- Curate visual reminders of your goals. Art, objects, or photos that evoke the feeling of your desire.
- Upgrade where you can. Even small changes — a plush towel, fresh flowers, a new mug you love — send signals of worthiness.

The Energetic Layer

- Scent: Use candles, essential oils, or fresh herbs to create an atmosphere that uplifts you.
- Sound: Curate playlists that match the emotional tone of your desires.
- Light: Natural light is a mood booster, but soft evening lighting can make you feel cozy and abundant.

The Symbolic Layer

Every item in your space carries a story. Ask yourself:

- Does this object represent the version of me I'm becoming?
- Does it connect me to my desired reality?

If something reminds you of struggle, fear, or a past version of yourself you've outgrown — let it go.

Your Home as a Manifestation Partner

When you align your space with your desires:

- Opportunities seem to "show up" more often.
- You feel more energized and inspired to take action.
- Your nervous system relaxes, because your surroundings feel safe and abundant.

Mini Practice: The Entryway Audit

Your front door and entryway are the first energetic touchpoint for everything entering your life.

- Clear the path so nothing blocks the flow of energy.
- Add something beautiful or symbolic of your desires where you'll see it first thing.
- Keep it fresh — swap items seasonally to signal movement and newness.

Journal Prompts

1. What spaces in my home feel magnetic and inspiring?
2. What spaces feel heavy or draining?
3. If my environment were a reflection of my desired reality, what would I add, remove, or change?

Affirmation

"My surroundings are a living vision board for my dreams. Every detail calls my desires toward me with ease."

Closing

When your environment is aligned with your desires, manifestation stops feeling like something you "do" and starts feeling like something you simply live inside of.

In the next chapter, we'll turn inward again and explore how to sustain elevated emotions — the energetic fuel that keeps your manifestation momentum strong from the inside out.

Step 6

Sustain Elevated Emotions That Fuel Manifestation from the Inside Out

If your thoughts are the blueprint, your emotions are the power source. Manifestation isn't only about thinking the right things — it's about feeling the reality of your desire as if it's already here.

When you sustain elevated emotions, you're not chasing your dreams… you're broadcasting them.

Why Emotion Is the Fuel

Thoughts alone are static.
Emotion is the current that makes those thoughts magnetic.

If you've ever walked into a room and immediately felt someone's joy or tension, you've experienced the truth: energy speaks before words.

When you consistently hold emotions like joy, love, gratitude, and excitement, you become a vibrational match for experiences that create more of those feelings.

The Science of Emotional Vibration

Your heart produces an electromagnetic field that can be measured several feet from your body. That field changes depending on your emotional state.

- High vibration emotions — gratitude, love, excitement — expand your field, making you more magnetic to aligned experiences.
- Low vibration emotions — fear, doubt, resentment — constrict your field, making it harder for your desires to connect with you.

This isn't about never feeling low emotions. It's about learning how to move through them and return to elevated states more quickly.

Elevated Emotions vs. Forced Positivity

Sustaining elevated emotions does not mean plastering on a fake smile or denying what you really feel.

It means:

- Allowing emotions to move through you instead of getting stuck.
- Returning to the emotional tone of your desired reality, again and again.
- Choosing to feed the feelings that align with your vision rather than the ones that drain your power.

The Five Core Elevated Emotions for Manifestation

1. Gratitude – Feeling thankful as if it's already done.
2. Love – For yourself, your life, and the people who cross your path.
3. Excitement – Anticipating your desires as if they're inevitable.
4. Trust – Releasing the need to control every detail.
5. Joy – Experiencing your now moment fully.

How to Sustain Elevated Emotions

- Start your day in the frequency. Before you check your phone or get out of bed, take 2–3 minutes to feel the emotion of already having your desire.
- Anchor emotions in your body. Use movement, breathwork, or posture shifts to "lock in" the feeling.
- Use sensory triggers. Scent, music, textures, or visuals can bring you back to your chosen state instantly.

- Rehearse scenarios. Imagine living your desire and linger in the emotional reality of it.

Mini Practice: Emotional Rehearsal

Close your eyes.

Imagine one of your desires as fully manifested. See it. Hear it. Feel it.

Then, deepen into the feeling — gratitude, joy, pride, peace.

Stay there for at least 90 seconds, allowing your nervous system to register it as safe and familiar.

Journal Prompts

1. Which emotions naturally lift my energy the most?
2. Which emotions tend to drain my momentum — and how can I release them faster?
3. What daily rituals can I create to sustain my desired state?

Affirmation

"I choose to feel the way my future self feels, now. My elevated emotions make my desires inevitable."

Closing

When your emotions are sustained at a higher vibration, you no longer have to force manifestation — it becomes an organic extension of who you are.

In the next chapter, we'll bridge the gap between the magical and the mundane as we explore how to live conscious creation in daily life, so that every choice and moment moves you toward your vision.

Step 7

Live Conscious Creation in Daily Life

Manifestation is not a ritual you do once a day.
It's a way of living.

The moment you understand that you are always creating — whether intentionally or not — you realize the power you hold. Every thought, choice, and interaction is shaping your reality. The question becomes: Are you creating consciously or by default?

Why Daily Life Is the True Practice

You can meditate, journal, and visualize all you want, but if you spend the rest of your day speaking fear, doubting your vision, or acting from lack, you dilute the signal.

Conscious creation is about carrying the frequency of your desires into your everyday actions — from how you answer an email to how you stir your morning coffee.

The 3 Pillars of Conscious Daily Creation

1. Awareness
   Pause often. Notice what you're thinking, feeling, and doing. Are they aligned with your future self or your past self?
2. Intention
   Start each activity with a simple intention: "I choose to bring love, clarity, and abundance to this call." It doesn't have to be dramatic. Small moments add up.
3. Alignment in Action
   Do the thing your desired self would do — even in small ways. If your future self values health, drink the extra glass of water. If

your future self is financially free, speak about money from a place of ease, not fear.

Micro-Moments That Matter

- The words you speak when talking to yourself in the mirror.
- How you handle unexpected challenges — as setbacks or as re-directions.
- The people, content, and environments you choose to engage with.
- How you treat others, especially when no one is watching.

Each choice is a vote for the reality you are building.

Making It Second Nature

When you live consciously, manifestation stops feeling like "something you do" and becomes "who you are."

That's when momentum becomes unstoppable — not because you're forcing it, but because you've made your desired vibration your default.

Journal Prompts

1. How am I unconsciously creating outcomes I don't want?
2. What is one way I can infuse more intention into my day tomorrow?
3. What would my desired self do differently today?

Affirmation

"Every moment is an opportunity to create. I choose to create with intention, love, and alignment."

Applying the Principles

You've just walked through the bridge from theory to embodiment. You now know how to harness belief, shift your identity, co-create with consciousness, detach and allow, design magnetic environments, sustain elevated emotions, and live as a conscious creator every single day.

Part Two was about becoming — rewiring your thoughts, aligning your actions, and building the emotional and energetic foundation for the life you want.

But understanding is only the first step.
The real magic happens when you practice

Part Three: Your Guided Journey

Practice: The Manifestation Blueprint

The Manifestation Blueprint is your personal map — the step-by-step framework you'll return to again and again whenever you want to call in something new, shift your energy, or realign with your vision.

You already have the knowledge from Parts One and Two. Now, this is about application.
Think of it like learning to swim: you've studied the strokes, the breathing, and the rhythm — but now, we're getting in the water.

Step 1

Clarify the Desire

You can't manifest what you can't name.
Write down exactly what you want in a clear, specific, and emotionally charged way.

Ask yourself:

- What do I truly want, not what I think I "should" want?
- How will I feel when I have it?
- Does this desire feel expansive in my body?

Pro Tip: If your body contracts or feels heavy, it's often a sign that the desire might be someone else's expectation or a "should" goal.

Step 2

Anchor Belief

Desire without belief is like planting a seed in dry soil.
You must water it with the certainty that it's already yours.

Practice:

- Write an "already done" journal entry as if you're living your desire now.
- Repeat affirmations that feel natural and believable.
- Spend two minutes a day visualizing the result with sensory detail.

Step 3

Embody Identity

You are not trying to become someone else — you are remembering the version of you that already exists.

Ask yourself daily:

- How would the me who already has this walk, talk, make decisions?
- What habits would they keep, and what would they release?

Then, start small:

- Upgrade one choice a day to match your future self.

Step 4

Co-Create with Consciousness

Manifestation is a partnership. You hold the vision, and the universe orchestrates the how.

- Stay open to unexpected opportunities.
- Follow intuitive nudges without overthinking.
- Treat synchronicities as green lights, not coincidences.

Step 5

Detach & Allow

Holding on too tightly strangles the flow.
Once the desire is set, relax your grip.

Practice:

- Set a "manifestation release ritual" — write your desire, bless it, then put it away.
- Focus on joy in the meantime.

Step 6

Create Magnetic Environments

Your surroundings are either reinforcing your old identity or your new one.

- Declutter and remove items that feel tied to your past.
- Add visuals, sounds, scents, and symbols that align with your desire.

Step 7

Sustain Elevated Emotions

The energy you carry is the frequency you transmit.

- Start your day with gratitude and appreciation.
- Engage in activities that naturally raise your mood.

Practice

21-Day Manifestation Challenge

Your three-week guided immersion into living the principles daily —
with short, focused actions that create big energetic shifts.

This challenge is designed to be doable, even on your busiest days. Each
step builds on the last, creating momentum and reinforcing belief until
manifestation becomes your default way of being.

Week 1 – Clarity & Belief

The focus here is on what you want and believing it's possible.

Day 1: Write Your Desire Statement

- Clearly define what you want. Keep it specific and emotionally charged.

Day 2: Sensory Visualization

- Spend 3–5 minutes visualizing your desire as if it's already yours
  — see, hear, feel it.

Day 3: Remove One Limiting Belief

- Write down a belief that says you can't have it. Then reframe it into an empowering one.

Day 4: Anchor in Gratitude

- List 5 things you're grateful for right now. Gratitude is the fastest frequency shifter.

Day 5: Act as If

- Make one choice today that your "already manifested" self would make.

Day 6: Future Self Journal Entry

- Write a page as if you're living your desire today.

Day 7: Belief Booster

- Read your desire statement out loud three times, morning and night, with full emotion.

Week 2 – Embodiment & Alignment

Now we move from thinking to being.

Day 8: Morning Identity Ritual

- Start the day asking, "How would my manifested self show up today?" and live it.

Day 9: Environmental Upgrade

- Remove one thing from your space that no longer matches the life you're creating.

Day 10: Follow a Nudge

- Take action on one intuitive idea today, no matter how small.

Day 11: Nervous System Reset

- Spend 5–10 minutes in breathwork, meditation, or grounding.

Day 12: Celebrate Mini-Wins

- Write down every small sign of progress you've noticed this week.

Day 13: Raise Your Frequency

- Do something purely because it lights you up.

Day 14: Inspired Action Day

- Take a bold step toward your desire — send the email, apply, make the call.

Week 3 – Surrender & Flow

We release control and let the universe do its part.

Day 15: Release Ritual

- Write your desire on paper, bless it, and place it somewhere special.

Day 16: Joy Practice

- Do one activity today that makes you lose track of time.

Day 17: Say Yes

- When an opportunity, compliment, or help comes your way —
  accept it.

Day 18: Clear Clutter Energy

- Spend 15 minutes decluttering a drawer, inbox, or workspace.

Day 19: Amplify Gratitude

- List 10 things you love about your life as it is right now.

Day 20: Receive Something

- It could be a gift, help, or even a compliment — receive without deflecting.

Day 21: Celebration Day

- Reflect on your 21 days. Write down all shifts, signs, wins, and how you now feel about your desire.

Look how far you've come!

The Universe Is Listening

There is a quiet magic in the way the Universe speaks — not in words, but in whispers.
It listens to every thought, every feeling, every intention you hold, and it responds not to what you *say* you want, but to what you *believe* is possible.

The moment you begin to align your energy — when your desire moves from the realm of wishful thinking into the vibration of certainty — the Universe leans in closer. It begins arranging people, opportunities, and "coincidences" that match your frequency. It listens through energy, not volume. You don't have to shout your dreams into the void; you only have to feel them into existence.

I remember when I first began to truly understand this. I was driving home one evening, wrestling with uncertainty about whether to take a leap in my career. I had been asking for a sign — something clear, something undeniable. As I drove, the song that came on the radio began with the exact words I had just spoken aloud to myself moments earlier. I laughed through tears, because I knew. It wasn't coincidence. It was the Universe answering back, saying, *I hear you.*

That's how it works — softly, often in ways you can miss if you're rushing through your day.
When your mind is still and your heart is open, the Universe has room to respond.

Signs That the Universe Is Listening

1. Synchronicities — The Meaningful Coincidences
Synchronicities are not random. They are the Universe's way of confirming alignment. When you think of someone and they suddenly text you, when an idea keeps appearing in different places, or when a door opens in perfect timing — those are responses to your frequency. Think of it as energetic conversation: you vibrate clarity, and the Universe replies, *I got the message.*

2. Repeating Numbers and Patterns
Numbers carry energy, and repeating sequences like 111, 222, 333, and

444 often appear when your intentions are being heard. Each pattern has its own resonance: 111 for new beginnings, 222 for balance, 333 for alignment, 444 for protection.

When you see them, pause and acknowledge them — say, *Thank you. I know you're listening.*

3. The Unexpected Detour

Sometimes the sign isn't a yes — it's a redirection. A job falls through, a plan shifts, or a delay appears out of nowhere. It's not rejection; it's realignment. The Universe knows the path you cannot yet see. Often, the "no" is simply making space for something better.

4. Emotional Resonance

You'll know the Universe is responding when peace begins to replace panic. That calm knowing in your gut — the one that feels like exhale — is the energetic confirmation that you're on the right path. Guidance often comes through feeling, not logic.

5. The Echo of Your Words

Have you ever noticed how quickly your words manifest? You speak of a trip, and suddenly a flight deal appears. You think about an idea, and someone mentions it the next day. The Universe mirrors your frequency through the conversations, signs, and moments that surround you.

When You Begin to Notice

Once you become aware that the Universe is listening, you'll start to live in conversation with it.

Every sign becomes sacred — the feather on your path, the timing of a phone call, the whisper in a lyric that feels written just for you.

One night, as I sat by the river watching the moon reflect on the water, I asked silently for reassurance — not about whether my dreams would come true, but whether I was still on the right path. Moments later, a single shooting star traced the sky, bright and undeniable. It was as if the Universe had said, *Keep going. I see you*

That's the beauty of it:
The more you trust that the Universe is listening, the more you begin to

hear it.

The signs become louder, the timing more perfect, and the alignment more effortless.

You stop chasing, and start conversing.
You stop doubting, and start co-creating.

Because the truth is —
the Universe has always been listening.
It's simply waiting for you to recognize that it has been answering all along.

The Universe is Always Listening.

Your Next Step

You've laid the foundation, shifted your energy, and acted from belief. Now you're ready for the next section of this book — the Workbook & Reflection Journal, where you'll integrate these practices into long-term habits and create a personal manifestation record you can return to for years.

Workbook & Reflection Journals

Weekly Alignment Check-In

Use these pages once a week to track your alignment and progress.

On a scale of 1–10, how aligned do I feel with my desires right now?

What felt most aligned this week?

Where did I feel resistance or doubt?

What action or shift moved me forward the most?

Manifestation Worksheets
A template for pulling everything together.

Clarity: What do I desire? Why?

Belief: What empowering beliefs support this?

Emotional Alignment: How will I feel when it's mine? How can I feel that now?

Inspired Action: What steps can I take today?

Detachment: How can I release control and trust the process?

Identity Alignment: Who do I need to become to live this desire?

Overcoming Resistance: What obstacles may show up, and how will I move through them?

Gratitude & Celebration Pages

Gratitude magnifies manifestation. Use these pages often.

Prompts:

Today I am grateful for...

This week I am celebrating...

A small win I want to acknowledge is...

One thing I appreciate about myself is...

Letter to My Future Self

Write a heartfelt letter to yourself as if your desires have already manifested.

Prompts:

- Describe your life now that your manifestations are here.
- Share how proud you are of yourself for becoming who you needed to be.
- Give your future self encouragement, love, and gratitude.

Closing Reflection Page

Looking Back on the Journey

What have I learned about myself through these principles?

How has my perspective on manifestation shifted?

Which practices will I continue daily, weekly, or monthly?

What desires have already started to unfold?

Reflection Practice for Affirmations

Affirmations are most powerful when you don't just say them — but when you *feel them*. This short practice will help you embody each affirmation so it becomes part of your energy and reality.

Step 1: Breathe

Close your eyes and take 3–5 slow, deep breaths. Inhale clarity, love, and possibility. Exhale doubt, fear, and resistance.

Step 2: Choose

Select one or two affirmations that resonate with you today. Trust your intuition — the right one will "light up" for you.

Step 3: Speak & Feel

Say your chosen affirmation out loud or silently. As you speak, imagine you already are what you are declaring. Feel the emotions — joy, gratitude, peace, certainty — in your body.

Step 4: Visualize

Picture yourself living the affirmation. See the details clearly — where you are, who you're with, how it feels, the smile on your face. Let it become real in your imagination.

Step 5: Anchor

Write your affirmation in a journal, or repeat it three times to seal it in. Carry it with you throughout the day, and return to it whenever you need to realign.

Affirmations for Clarity

- I Am clear in my vision for my life.
- I Am certain about the direction I am moving in.
- I Am aligned with my highest purpose.
- I Am open to receiving divine guidance with ease.
- I Am focused on what truly matters.
- I Am intentional with my thoughts and actions.
- I Am releasing confusion and embracing clarity.
- I Am seeing my goals vividly in my mind's eye.
- I Am choosing simplicity over distraction.
- I Am confident in my decisions.
- I Am aware of the opportunities before me.
- I Am guided toward the right people, places, and resources.
- I Am shining a light on my next best step.
- I Am focused and grounded in the present moment.
- I Am free from doubt and hesitation.
- I Am creating space for clarity to flow through me.
- I Am clear in my intentions and direction.
- I Am always guided by truth and inner wisdom.
- I Am focused, calm, and certain about my path.
- I Am the author of my story, and I see it unfolding clearly.

Affirmations for Belief

- I Am confident that my dreams are possible.
- I Am rooted in unwavering faith.
- I Am worthy of the life I desire.
- I Am aligned with the belief that the universe supports me.
- I Am certain that my vision is already unfolding.
- I Am choosing belief over doubt.
- I Am empowered by my inner knowing.
- I Am capable of achieving all that I set my heart to.
- I Am trusting the process of manifestation.
- I Am believing in my power to create.
- I Am sure of my path and my purpose.
- I Am magnetizing abundance through belief.
- I Am worthy of miracles.
- I Am fueled by faith, not fear.
- I Am holding the vision even when I cannot see the evidence.
- I Am secure in the truth that my desires are on their way.
- I Am strengthening my belief each day.
- I Am choosing to believe in limitless possibilities.
- I Am certain that everything is working out for my highest good.
- I Am the evidence of belief made real.

Affirmations for Emotional Alignment

- I Am tuned to the frequency of joy.
- I Am aligned with love, peace, and gratitude.
- I Am in harmony with the emotions of my desires.
- I Am choosing thoughts that feel good.
- I Am connected to the energy of abundance.
- I Am raising my vibration daily.
- I Am a match for the feelings of fulfillment.
- I Am flowing with ease and grace.
- I Am grounded in positivity and peace.
- I Am releasing low energies and stepping into joy.
- I Am choosing to feel now what I wish to manifest.
- I Am embodying happiness in the present moment.
- I Am letting gratitude overflow in my heart.
- I Am tuned into the frequency of success.
- I Am aligned with the feelings of love and freedom.
- I Am radiating high vibrational energy.
- I Am at peace with my journey.
- I Am magnetizing all that resonates with my joy.
- I Am aligned emotionally with my vision.
- I Am a vessel of positivity and light.

Affirmations for Inspired Action

- I Am ready to act on divine nudges.
- I Am moving with courage and purpose.
- I Am inspired to take steps that align with my vision.
- I Am guided toward the right actions at the right time.
- I Am fearless in pursuing my dreams.
- I Am proactive in co-creating my reality.
- I Am motivated by clarity and purpose.
- I Am walking in alignment with my higher self.
- I Am willing to act boldly on my intuition.
- I Am choosing progress over perfection.
- I Am always taking steps forward, no matter how small.
- I Am listening to my inner wisdom and acting on it.
- I Am aligned with opportunities that move me closer to my goals.
- I Am excited to act on inspired ideas.
- I Am committed to taking consistent action.
- I Am courageous in stepping outside my comfort zone.
- I Am choosing inspired action over idle waiting.
- I Am guided to take aligned steps with ease.
- I Am supported in every action I take.

Affirmations for Detachment

- I Am free from the need to control outcomes.
- I Am releasing attachment to timing and details.
- I Am open to miracles in unexpected ways.
- I Am letting go with trust and faith.
- I Am at peace with the unfolding of life.
- I Am surrendering to divine timing.
- I Am trusting the process completely.
- I Am free from worry and doubt.
- I Am calm as I wait for what is mine.
- I Am releasing resistance with ease.
- I Am open to receiving in ways beyond my imagination.
- I Am allowing space for magic to happen.
- I Am detached yet aligned with my desires.
- I Am certain without needing proof.
- I Am content in the now while expecting more.
- I Am releasing pressure and embracing flow.
- I Am confident even without control.
- I Am surrendering outcomes to the universe.
- I Am free and light in my waiting.
- I Am unattached yet fully aligned.

Affirmations for Identity Alignment

- I Am the version of myself who already has what I desire.
- I Am embodying my highest self.
- I Am aligning my choices with who I truly am.
- I Am living in full alignment with my vision.
- I Am stepping into my future self daily.
- I Am the energy of success, abundance, and love.
- I Am already the person I aspire to become.
- I Am living my identity with authenticity.
- I Am aligned with the values of my true self.
- I Am walking in the reality I have chosen.
- I Am integrating new beliefs into who I am.
- I Am choosing habits that match my future self.
- I Am embodying abundance now.
- I Am stepping fully into my power.
- I Am congruent with my words, thoughts, and actions.
- I Am a reflection of the reality I am manifesting.
- I Am choosing to live as if it is already done.
- I Am aligned with the identity of a manifestor.
- I Am the creator of my destiny.
- I Am living in my chosen identity with ease.

Affirmations for Overcoming Resistance

- I Am free from self-doubt and fear.
- I Am letting go of limiting beliefs.
- I Am releasing all resistance to my desires.
- I Am open to receiving without struggle.
- I Am breaking through every barrier with ease.
- I Am worthy of having what I want.
- I Am replacing fear with faith.
- I Am flowing with trust instead of resistance.
- I Am choosing thoughts that support me.
- I Am dissolving all blocks in my path.
- I Am confident in moving forward.
- I Am letting go of what no longer serves me.
- I Am free from old patterns and stories.
- I Am aligned with ease, flow, and possibility.
- I Am ready to receive without resistance.
- I Am fearless in releasing the past.
- I Am strong enough to overcome any obstacle.
- I Am choosing to align, not to resist.
- I Am surrendering all tension and fear.
- I Am free, open, and ready for what is mine.

•

Closing: I Am Manifesting

Here is a blended set of affirmations across all 7 principles. These can serve as your **final anchoring practice** — a reminder that everything you need is already within you.

- I Am clear in my vision and direction.
- I Am rooted in belief that all things are possible.
- I Am aligned with the emotions of my desires.
- I Am inspired to take bold, aligned action.
- I Am free from attachment and open to miracles.
- I Am embodying the identity of my highest self.
- I Am releasing all resistance and stepping into flow.
- I Am worthy of abundance, love, and success.
- I Am guided by inner wisdom and divine timing.
- I Am creating my reality with intention and power.
- I Am aligned with joy, gratitude, and peace.
- I Am open to receiving beyond my imagination.
- I Am the author of my destiny.
- I Am magnetizing opportunities, love, and prosperity.
- I Am living as if my desires are already fulfilled.
- I Am supported by the universe in every moment.
- I Am choosing faith over fear.
- I Am fully aligned with my purpose.
- I Am grateful for all that is, and all that is coming.
- I Am a powerful creator, and everything I desire is already mine.

Acknowledgments

Writing this book has been a profoundly personal and transformative experience—one that could not have come to life without the unwavering support, love, and encouragement of so many cherished people.

To my sons, Kai and Skyler—you are my heart and my inspiration. Watching you embrace life with purpose and joy reminds me every day of the incredible power we each possess to shape our own destinies. I hope this book serves as a reminder that you can create the life you imagine.

To my husband, Alex—thank you for always believing in me. Your steadfast love, encouragement, and quiet strength have grounded me through every dream and every chapter. I am endlessly grateful for you.

To my mama.. thank you for always encouraging me to dream big dreams. Love you so much.

To my family and closest friends—your faith in me has meant everything. Your laughter, support, and kind words have lifted me up, especially during moments of doubt.

To my readers and fellow manifestors—thank you for saying yes to your dreams and for daring to pursue your truest selves. Your courage and willingness to grow make this world a brighter place. I see you, I believe in you, and I am honored to walk this path alongside you.

And finally, to the universe—for every sign, synchronicity, intuitive nudge, and moment of magic that has guided me here. I trust you now more deeply than ever.

With Love & Gratitude, Christine

ABOUT THE AUTHOR

Christine Zanjanipour is a creator, entrepreneur, and visionary voice in the world of conscious living and leadership. She is the founder of **Details Matter Books**, a boutique publishing imprint that celebrates intentional design, elevated storytelling, and the art of living with purpose.

The author of multiple lifestyle and personal growth works—including *The Manifest Principles*, *The Manifest Principles in Business*, *I Am Because I Say I Am*, *The Staring Game*, *The Hostess with the Mostest*, *Flourishing Bread Co.*, and *Yummers!*—Christine writes for those who believe that clarity, belief, alignment, and inspired action can transform not only lives, but entire organizations.

With over two decades of experience in business development and data-driven marketing, Christine has guided leading brands, coached high-performing teams, and helped companies bring consciousness into the workplace. Her unique approach blends strategic insight with the energetic power of manifestation—bridging the worlds of logic and intuition, data and energy, purpose and performance.

Beyond her books, Christine is the creative force behind several lifestyle ventures that reflect her passion for artistry, hospitality, and the joy of everyday beauty—from artisan bread and olive oil to elevated travel and mindful living.

She lives with her husband, Alex, along the Roaring Fork River in Glenwood Springs, Colorado, where the mountains inspire her to ski, bake, write, dream, and create experiences that remind others of what's possible when passion meets presence.

Christine believes in living deliberately, leading energetically, and noticing the beauty in every detail—because, in business and in life, **details always matter.**

Let's Stay Connected

If you'd like to continue the conversation — through workshops, manifestation coaching, or conscious business retreats — you can find me at:

Follow The Manifest Principles:

Instagram: https://www.instagram.com/themanifestprinciples

Facebook: https://www.facebook.com/themanifestprinciples

www.DetailsMatterBooks.com

I'd love to hear how this work moves through you and your company. Your stories, your insights, and your transformations keep this energy alive.

Because the more we share, the more we expand — together.

With clarity, belief, and a little bit of magic —

DETAILS
MATTER
BOOKS